*Affirmative
and Spiritual
to the Sacre*

Beyond Inspiration

Marie Jiménez-Beaumont

Beyond Inspiration

*No part of this book may be used or reproduced in
any manner whatsoever without written permission
of the publisher, or author.*

*All rights reserved
Copyright © 2011
Marie Jiménez-Beaumont*

Published in the U.S.A.

ISBN-13
978-1466391444

ISBN-10
1466391448

Dedication

This book is dedicated to loved ones who are part of the tapestry of my life:

My soulmate, Phil, who once intuitively told me, before we fell in love, that, "a little bird told me that your life is about to change." Little did we know he was going to be the catalyst of that change. It's been an amazing spiritual and human journey where love and total acceptance of one another prevails. I am deeply grateful and humbled for this blessing in my life.

My sister Norma and her late son Omar, who left us too quickly at the tender age of 18. Both my sister and nephew have been a sacred part of my journey and of unconditional love.

And to my older nephew Andrew, whose spirit of adventure and courage I admire.

TABLE OF CONTENTS

Dedication – *3*

Introduction – *9*

Part 1
Affirmative Prayers – *13*
A New Day – *14*
Prayer for Attracting a Soulmate – *15*
For Inner Peace – *17*
To Feel the Presence of Divinity – *18*
For the World – *19*
Gratitude Prayer *21*
Prayer for Forgiveness – *22*
Prayer for Protection – *23*
Financial Freedom – *24*
Prayer for Wisdom – *25*
For Releasing Addictions or Habits – *26*
Prayer for Employment – *27*
Self-Love – *28*
Prayer for Clarity of Mind – *29*
Prayer for Healing of Conflict – *31*
Prayer for Willpower – *32*
For Joy – *33*
A Prayer for Inspiration – *34*
A Cleansing Prayer – *35*
Our Children – *37*
Freedom from Worry – *38*
Abundance Prayer – *39*
Celebrating Life – *40*
Gratitude for the Internet – *41*
A Prayer for Pets– *43*

TABLE OF CONTENTS

A Prayer for Patience with Intentions –	 44
For Courage –	 45
In Times of Grief –	 47
For a Happy Home –	 48
Evening Prayer –	 49

Part 2
Spiritual Musings –

	 51
Come Empty –	 52
Purpose –	 52
Love Embraces All -	 53
The Naked Truth –	 55
Soul's Longing –	 55
Trusting the Perfection of the Universe –	 56
Recognizing the World is But an Illusion -	 57
Infinity's Touch –	 59
Listening to the Whispers –	 61
On Having a Hearing Challenge –	 62
Recapturing Our Childlike Joy –	 63
Surrender and Release –	 64
Compassion – A Lesson for the Day –	 65
Death – A Temporary Separation –	 68
I am Your Angel –	 69
Spirit Speaking –	 71
Loss of Child –	 71
Openings and Connections –	 72
Death and Rebirth -	 72
Impermanence –	 73
Transformation –	 73
Behind the Veil –	 75
Flying Free –	 75
Closure	 76
Nature's Lessons	 79

TABLE OF CONTENTS

Part 3
Inspire My Day Affirmations – *81*
Attachments – *82*
Doing what I Love – *82*
Creating My Day – *83*
Magnificence – *83*
Wholeness – *83*
Wisdom – *85*
Honoring Life – *85*
Abundance – *85*
The Breath of Life – *87*
Magic of Life – *87*
Supportive People – *87*
Allowing Joy – *88*
I am Calm – *88*
Committing to Goals – *88*
Healthy Body – *89*
Unique Divine Expression – *89*
Higher Voice – *89*
Infinite Field of Possibilities – *91*
Forgiveness – *91*
In the Moment – *91*
Self-Trust – *93*
Mind, Body and Spirit Renewal – *93*
Freedom from Limitations – *95*
Greatness of Spirit – *95*
Clear Path – *95*
Bounty of the Universe – *96*
Mind and Heart Agreeing – *96*
Releasing Limiting Thoughts – *96*
Miracles – *97*
Self-Love – *97*

TABLE OF CONTENTS

Part 4
Soothe Your Soul Meditations 99
Stillness – 99
Nature Speaks – 100
The Eagles' Gift – 100
Expressions of One Source – 100
Simplifying – 101
We Are Love – 101
Beauty's Love Song – 101
Gratitude – 103
Present Moment – 103
God's Creative Expression – 103
Dance and Dancer – 104
Soul's Prompting – 104
Impermanent World – 104
Ego's Need – 105
Yielding Heart – 105
Equanimity – 105
Life's Song – 106
Surrender – 106
Experiencing the God in You – 106
Duality – 107
Kindness - 107
Greatness of our Spirit - 107
The Ocean's Gift – 109
Reflection – 109
Divine Unfolding – 109
Cosmic Dance – 111
Silencing Mind's Chatter – 111
Love – 111

TABLE OF CONTENTS

Appendix

Beyond Inspiration Notebook - *112*

Spiritual and Inspirational Resources - *118*

About the Author - *121*

Introduction

On a cool autumn day, I was sitting in my office thinking and writing. Music was playing in the background and a garden filled with water fountains faced my window. To my right, a scented candle was burning near pictures of my loved ones who have passed on. And next to those pictures was a statue of Archangel Michael that has accompanied me over many miles and many years as I relocated from one end of the USA to the other. Even when I expanded my ideas of what the nature of reality and God is, I have kept this statue. It's my connection to a higher force, one that I may not see, but that is there for me at all times. Next to my office, my mate was peacefully writing in his own office. Life can have so much beauty, such as the beauty I was seeing and feeling in that moment, but then there are also moments of loss – not only of loved ones, but of a relationship, health, job, money, home – that can hurt us deeply and shake the core of our being.

This is what life can be at times: the contrast between the experiences that fill us with peace and the ones that challenge that peace. I have learned that shifting our focus so we see the sacredness in everything we do, from the air we breathe to the food we eat and the love we give, honors our individual existence on this planet and strengthens our awareness of the Presence of God. This Presence would be life itself, as all that is on this planet has the essence of God permeating it. Through having a reverence for life, we can transcend our pain.

In living life with an appreciation of our sacredness, we learn to honor the sacredness of others. This opens our hearts to seeing the perfection and beauty that is within each and every one, no matter where we are in our human expression, as each person/soul has lessons to learn. The physicality of this reality will end one day, but the real substance of our being, our souls, will live and shine forever; it's a stepping into another portal, a continuing dance with the energy of God.

Imagine a world where we all honored ourselves and others, not from the filters of our minds, but from the love within our hearts and souls. The world would, indeed, be a paradise since the human need to judge and harm would dissolve.

The sages of old have said, while holding their pressed hands in front of their hearts or third eye, "Namaste," which means, "I honor the spirit in you that is in me." I continue to honor myself and be grateful for my existence, here and in the world beyond, and encourage you to honor yourselves as God's divine creation.

It is my hope that the words in this book will create a sense of the sacredness in your life. Words and thoughts put to positive use have power – the power to uplift, to inspire, to heal. With this in mind, we need to take responsibility for the words we use with others whether in written or oral form, and above all, with our self-talk. Often, "we become what we think." This is not only a law of attraction statement; our brains' and bodies' health responds to our constant self-talk. Reading positive prayers or spiritual thoughts will help raise our focus and vibration, both mentally and spiritually.

What follows in this book is a compilation of spiritual (but non-religious, so it fits all paths) affirmative prayers, affirmations, and spiritual musings to keep you company and create a dialog within you that is positive and filled with the sacred beauty and grace of Spirit.

Namaste,
 Marie

Affirmative Prayers

Affirmative Prayers

Affirmative praying recognizes the Omniscience, Omnipotence, and Omnipresence of God/Spirit and the realization we are One with Spirit.

With affirmative prayers, instead of begging for an outcome, we establish an inner communion with the Divine and focus on a positive outcome. The prayer generally ends with "It is so" or "And so it is" as a declaration that we have the faith that a Higher Source is working in unity with our intentions. This powerful method has its basis in the teachings of New Thought, which is, in turn, the foundation of the current human potential movement.

The beauty of affirmative praying is all paths can use this form of prayer without denying their religion or spiritual inclinations. Consciousness/God is available to all in whatever method suits us best. The one commonality shared by all humans who turn to prayer is the wish to create a sacred space where the challenges in their lives will find a resolution, where clarity of mind will take place, or the yearning to help others will receive divine intervention.

Establishing a routine of prayer and contemplation means creating a quiet space in your life where you are consciously opening your mind and heart to an inner communion with the divine. The benefits are many-fold; your spiritual connection is strengthened, and clarity can arise as you take a moment to pray and surrender your burden to the divine in you. Renewed energy and the gift of grace become available as we continue the path of becoming instruments of God.

May peace, love, and the beauty of the grace of Spirit enter your life as you enter the energy of the words shared here.

A New Day

As I start a new day, I pray
that love, wisdom, and clarity guide me
in all my ways.
May I see each and every person
who crosses my path
through the eyes
of non-judgment and
a heart that understands
we are all equally an expression of God.
On this new day, I affirm that I am releasing
the problems of yesterday and fears
of the future, so I will be in the moment
appreciating the sacredness of life,
the opportunity to learn, to grow,
and to release anything
that blocks the joyful
Light of my being!
And so it is!

Marie Jiménez-Beaumont

Prayer for Attracting a Soulmate

Dear God/Source/Creator,
I know that the essence of who we all are is Love.
My body, my soul, the very air that
I breathe is infused with Your Love.
I open my mind, my heart, my spirit and let go
of fears or unreasonable expectations.
I affirm that my energy field will attract
the perfect soulmate into my life,
one who is respectful, caring, loving
and supportive in our shared journey in life.
As I release these words into Infinity,
it is done!
Thank you for the answer to my prayer!
And so it is. Amen!

Beyond Inspiration

For Inner Peace

Dear God,
The source of all seen and unseen—
I am willing to let go of all
thoughts, attachments, and fears
that rob me of my peace of mind,
but I need the Grace and Stillness of Spirit
to permeate my entire being.
Send angels on earth, seen and unseen,
to assist me in my daily life
and my nightly dreams,
so I can see with clarity
what I need to release and
have the courage to let go
of what no longer works
for my well-being and inner peace.
Dear God, I am willing to be a
channel of your peace.
It is so! Amen!

To Feel the Presence of Divinity

*I want to feel your Presence
every single day and night.
I want to walk knowing I am never alone.
I realize that I am That,
I am Divinity manifested,
but I get lost in the world of illusion
and think I am only the identity
of the name I was given at birth
and the personality I express.
I am aware I am much more
than this physical body
or the thoughts that I have,
but I want to remember
I am God in expression
And that your Presence
is always in me.
And so it is!*

Marie Jiménez-Beaumont

For the World

Where there is hatred, let there be love.
Where there is hunger, let there be nourishment.
Where there is suffering, let there be relief.
Where wars are being fought, let there be peace.
Where there is prejudice, let there be unity.
Where sickness is, let there be healing.
Where there is ignorance, let there be understanding.
Where there is religious or spiritual intolerance,
Let there be acceptance.
May love, peace, and wholeness prevail on Earth!
And so it is! Amen.

Gratitude Prayer

I am grateful for a brand new day!
For the clouds with their funny shapes,
For the sunshine and the rain.
I am grateful for food and shelter,
for my health and good mind.
I am grateful for my loved ones and friends,
the ones who are still with me
and the ones who were once in my life.
I am grateful for the Presence of God/Spirit
in all my affairs!
I am grateful for a heart that feels
warmth, love, and a deep appreciation
for the blessings of life!
It is so. Amen!

Prayer for Forgiveness

Today I am willing to be in a place of forgiveness.
I let go of all resentments that are
heavy burdens that weigh me down,
and like dark clouds that hide the
sunshine that could be in my day.
I let go, forgive myself and others,
as we all do the best we can
from our level of awareness,
and we all can grow from our human lessons.
I let go, replace resentment, hurts, and anger
in my heart with the sweet nectar of love.
The past is gone,
the present is all I have.
I rejoice in finally setting myself free!
And so it is!

Marie Jiménez-Beaumont

Beyond Inspiration

Prayer for Protection

Dear Spirit,
On this blessed day that you have created,
I ask for angels to surround me
and my loved ones.
May we be protected from all harm!
May divine energy keep the path clear,
transmuting all darkness into light.
May divine light surround our bodies,
our minds, our souls -
Forming a brilliant, protective shield
of divine energy!
On this blessed day, dear Spirit,
I give thanks for the sacred connection
with the protective power of Your Divinity.
And so it is!

Financial Freedom

This is an abundant universe that can provide
for every citizen of the world.
I let go of all thoughts of lack!
I trust that whatever I am currently experiencing
is a movement toward abundance.
I refuse to participate in the mass consciousness of
fear
that contributes to the energy of lack.
I let go of all ideas that I must struggle to provide
for my needs and those of my loved ones.
I willingly align in the consciousness of
abundant, joyful, and healthy living!
As I raise my focus, I in turn serve the planet
with my healthy thoughts of abundance
as we are all connected and affect one another.
And so it is. Amen!

Marie Jiménez-Beaumont

Prayer for Wisdom

As I move through the journey of my life
I pray for wisdom in everything I do.
From the words I choose to express
to the choices and actions that I take-
May they be tempered with
love, understanding, and a clarity
that comes from a full heart,
and a mind that is in silent repose.
May wisdom continue to guide me
every day, every hour, every moment,
so I can live a life fully blessed
in this sacred dance we call life.
And so it is!

For Releasing Addictions or Habits

I give it up!
I surrender this habit/addiction of _____
(describe the issue)
to the Infinite Mind/God/Source.
Every time I desire to sabotage my well being
by indulging in this habit/addiction,
I do not focus on it; I simply surrender it to God!
By taking the focus away from what I no longer want in my life,
it loses its grip and power over me from lack of attention.
What I cease to feed loses energy and
it is no longer in my life and space.
Whenever the desire creeps up again
I repeat: "I surrender, let go, let God and I am free!"
And so it is! Amen.

Marie Jiménez-Beaumont

Beyond Inspiration

Prayer for Employment

*In a planet that is always growing, changing and
where there are needs to be fulfilled,
there is opportunity of work for all.
I wish to have the security and provide financially
for my loved ones and myself.
May I be guided to work that I love.
May I be surrounded in an atmosphere
of cooperation and respect.
May I be embraced by calm and confidence
during interviews and do so well
that I will be hired and gainfully employed!
I let go of the fear of staying unemployed
and trust in the bounty of the universe!
Thank you for the answer to this prayer!
And so it is! Amen.*

Self-Love

*What I attract into my experience,
the way I express my life,
is largely a reflection of how I feel about myself.
I am a divine being in human form,
no less than the trees and the stars.
I have many values, traits, and qualities
that are uniquely mine and
a gift to myself and to the world.
I love and appreciate every part of
my body, my mind, and my soul,
and see the perfection and beauty of my being.
I honor the gift of my life
and choose to live with a deep gratitude and love
for self and for others.
And so it is. Amen!*

Marie Jiménez-Beaumont

Prayer for Clarity of Mind

Dear Spirit/God/Source/Mother Earth,
A clear and steady mind
is what I yearn for,
as I am confused at the moment
with dark thoughts and feelings
that block the light of my being.
Clarity, I understand, comes from the
Stillness within me, which is my true nature.
I pray that I be guided to tap
into this Eternal Stillness that reflects as a pool of
calmness, serenity, peace, and love in my life.
As I reconnect to the Eternal Stillness within,
a natural alignment with my higher wisdom takes place.
I pray that in this state of alignment I be guided
to make empowering decisions and choices
so that my life becomes a clear source
of joy, free from limitation.
And so it is!

Beyond Inspiration

Prayer for Healing of Conflict

Dear Infinite Love/God,
I am in emotional pain right now.
I feel angry, sad, and justified in my self-defense,
even if a part of me realizes all these petty
arguments are only of the ego/mind -
They are only imaginary perceptions
in the one I am in conflict with and myself.
Help me to see the unified energy
and essence of love in the beloved, for we are all one.
The minute I surrender this conflict to Love
and let it go from my mind and heart
the conflict dissolves in me.
I cannot control another, but I can
choose what I carry within,
and I choose harmony, peace,
and forgiveness for self and others.
May peace, love, and understanding prevail!
It is so. Amen!

Prayer for Willpower

When I set my mind to achieve a goal
I often give up before I see it through.
I get discouraged thinking, "What is the use?"
But a part of me is willing to try again!
I pray that my mind will work
in concert with my willingness.
This time I am open to being in the flow,
focusing on my intention
and the sense of joyful accomplishment I will feel.
I let go of worries of how long it may take...
or attention to any discomfort I may feel
while working to see its fulfillment.
I pray for the strength and will power
to move toward present and future goals!
I am grateful for inner shifts that are taking place
in my mind and heart that
allow for the answer to this prayer
to take place in my life.
And so it is!

Marie Jiménez-Beaumont

Beyond Inspiration

For Joy

There is an Infinite Presence and the natural Law of Attraction
that irresistibly keeps on creating without end.
This Infinite Presence draws to me all that brings
me health, love, friendship, happiness, prosperity, and
all that I need to have a joyful life experience.
I completely trust in this Presence that is
in me, around me, with me, as me, at all times.
While acknowledging this Presence,
I release anything in me such as fears, doubts, or negativity
that obstruct the experience of joy in my life.
I let any clouds of negativity disperse
in the higher vibration and light of joy.
Freedom and joy are mine today!
I proclaim I am being guided at all times
by a Higher Wisdom and Love
and, therefore, enter into
a fulfilling dance with life.
And so it is!

A Prayer for Inspiration

Today I walk in the path of inspiration.
My mind is a radiant vessel of illumination
that brings forth from the depths
of my heart and soul the expression of
my God-given creative abilities.
My path is governed by a Higher Source.
I am in the perfect flow of Creation
and I know with a calm certainty
of where the direction of my ideas,
thoughts, and decisions should be.
My path is filled with joy and anticipation.
I bask in the radiance of all my good
and give thanks for the bounty of the Universe!
And so it is!

Marie Jiménez-Beaumont

Beyond Inspiration

A Cleansing Prayer

The Infinite Love of God
surges in me and throughout my entire body
cleansing and revitalizing every
tissue, cell, and organ in my body.
The Light of God clears all blocks
in my mind and energy field,
allowing me to be a clear vessel where
the highest good shall come to me
and the highest good shall go from me.
The Peace of God infuses me
with love, wisdom, clarity
and the peace that passes all understanding.
I am eternally grateful for the answer to
these affirmative words.
And so it is!

Our children are the hope for the future.

Our Children

Our children are the hope for the future
born in a world that is often filled with strife and divisiveness
brought on by mankind's misalignment with its higher nature.
May the Divine inner spark within these innocents
protect them and guide them as they
start their journey in this world.
May the inner spark within each child
ignite into a collective awakening as they become adults.
May this spark help to bring the light of love and understanding
into the hearts of every man and woman in this world.
May the children of the world show the way
and usher humanity at last into a brand new world.
So it is. Amen!

Freedom from Worry

*I refuse to indulge in thoughts
that take me out of my inner balance.
I have full confidence that my Inner Divinity
is guiding me moment by moment,
and trust everything is working
for my highest good.
As I breathe in calm,
I breathe out fear.
As I breathe in harmony,
I set myself free from the worries of the past.
I am grateful for the power of these affirmative words,
and now can move forward confident and serene.
And so it is!*

Marie Jiménez-Beaumont

Abundance Prayer

*No matter what the circumstances are now,
I choose to be open to a joyful and vibrant
Never-ending flow of abundance in my life!
My thoughts are magnetic and uplifting and
are guiding me to create an existence where
the bounty of good surrounds me in every area of my life!
My relationships are filled with harmony and love.
My health is perfect, and I am blessed with abundant
energy.
My finances are always prospering, allowing me to
enjoy financial freedom and the ability to give back to
the world.
I am so confident and trusting of the abundance of the
universe
that I now can relax into a state of gratitude
for the harvest of good in my world!
And so it is!*

Celebrating Life

I celebrate the gift of life!
The wonder of all creation,
the children's laughter,
our human capacity to love
and the tenderness, compassion,
courage, and nobility that
mankind has shown in times
of sadness and despair of a fellow human being.
I celebrate the trees, the oceans,
the starry skies, and the critters large and small!
I rejoice that I am part of the dance of life,
for the air that I breathe, and, above
all, for the opportunity to create a life
of perfect peace and love.
And so it is!

Marie Jiménez-Beaumont

Beyond Inspiration

Gratitude for the Internet

The Internet is a window to the world
that has given me the opportunity
to connect to my brothers and sisters
around the globe – I have found
our similarities surpass our differences,
and for this opportunity of kinship and
understanding, I am deeply grateful.
I am grateful for the vast information at my fingertips,
and for the learning, entertainment,
and creativity that have enhanced my world.
I am grateful for the job and business opportunities –
past, present, or future – that I otherwise would not
have available
had the Internet not been invented in this generation.
May this amazing technology continue to grow and
enhance the lives of all and be put to positive use!
And so it is!

May all our creatures, small and large be treated with kindness, love and appreciation.

A Prayer for Pets

Our pets are companions for many humans
who respond to the master's
love and caring and even negativity
with unconditional love.
May all our creatures, small and large,
be treated with kindness, love, and appreciation
for the gift of their presence in our lives.
May any cruelty happening now toward
our animals be erased from the consciousness
of this planet and be replaced
with respect and love for
all life forms on our planet!
And so it is!

A Prayer for Patience with Intentions

I know that when I live from a place
of inner stillness and love,
life becomes a source of
graceful flow and patience.
I understand that everything that
manifests into being
comes from a seed,
and my seed is my intention
released to a greater Consciousness.
I trust that all my goals and my intentions
are blossoming in their right timing
and according to my Highest Good.
And so it is!

Marie Jiménez-Beaumont

For Courage

Today I surrender all fear of any
challenges I need to face or resolve
by staying centered within
my own inner divine power.
I am guided with
courage and wisdom
in all my affairs,
and a sweet calm comes over me.
I am aware everything
comes and goes in this
world of temporary form,
so this moment, too, shall pass.
All is well in my world!
And so it is!

As I release the constriction of suffering, my soul moves on with a newfound release and strength.

In Times of Grief

My heart is heavy with sorrow
and cannot see the light at the end,
but a deeper part of myself
knows through the tears
that the only way through this pain
is by surrendering, letting go, and letting God.
I am willing to let the Love from
the Divine Being that created me
embrace me and open my soul and heart.
I am willing to let angels, seen and unseen,
assist me as we all are connected.
As I release the constriction of suffering,
my soul moves on with a
newfound release and strength.
And so it is. Amen!

For a Happy Home

*My home is my sanctuary and shelter,
and I affirm it is a place of
love, nurturing, and peace.
Every nook and cranny of my home is
surrounded by the pure white Light of Spirit
and all disharmony or any lack being experienced
is transmuted into the Light,
restoring perfect balance and joy.
My home is a safe sanctuary where the bounty of
the universe enters and enriches and nourishes
my life and that of my loved ones.
And so it is! Amen.*

Marie Jiménez-Beaumont

Evening Prayer

Thank you, Dear Creator
for the gift of today:
for the sun that brought light
and for the rain that
nourished your world,
and for the setting of the sun
that brings a blanket of soothing
darkness into the evening.
Thank you for the love
that still prevails in this world of form,
for the hope of humanity.
Thank you for the wonders
and miracles that still appear on our planet,
and for the courage and strength for those
who are experiencing suffering.
As I lay me down to sleep,
I am grateful for your Presence
throughout the day
and for the opportunity
to choose the higher road
in the use of my precious mind
and the nurturing of my soul.
And so it is. Amen!

Spiritual Musings

Spiritual Musings

When we embark on a spiritual journey that we hope will answer the questions we have about God and the meaning of life and death, we often seek knowledge or inspiration from the books we read, the online community we may socialize in, our place of worship, or lectures from teachers wiser than we are, hoping to find a pearl of wisdom that will impact us and, perhaps, change our lives. We learn not only from the sage ones, but also from our everyday encounters, including the homeless man in our path. Others, in turn, also learn from us. In the end, we may become aware that the answers we have been seeking are within us, and if we learn to silence the mind, we will see a glimpse of Truth.

It matters not to Consciousness/God/Source if the lessons are difficult or joyful ones, not because there isn't love, but because Consciousness/God/Source seeks to experience through each one of us and make Itself aware to us, so we will see the face of God in ourselves and in all of Creation.

These short spiritual musings were borne out of moments of inspiration and spiritual chats in the park with my soul mate. I am a work in progress. What I believe in today may change in the next moment when simple love and truth may touch me and pierce the veil of illusion that kept me from seeing transcendent truth.

Come Empty

We too should make ourselves empty, that the great soul of the universe may fill us with its breath." – Laurence Binyon (1869-1943)

If you are to be a friend, come empty. Come empty of ideas of what others should or should not be, how they must look, how they should dress, or how their life or connection to God ought to be.

Come empty of judgments and ignorance, which we all have learned, for they create separation in the world and give birth to the made-up stories of one another. Come empty and you will find that hearts have a way of softening, relaxing, and opening like a bud in the springtime, ready to be filled and to savor the moment. By being empty we can sow the seeds of brotherhood in mankind.

Purpose

"Everything that lives, lives not alone, not for itself." – William Blake (1757-1827)

If I were told that there is not a real purpose to life, I would say, we are here to somehow add to the love and balance of the world. All of nature is solitary, yet interconnected; we weave a web that affects one another in perfect symmetry, even if our mind may tell us otherwise. If I but touch another person's life through my actions or words, or add to the collective consciousness by my own evolution, I have fulfilled my purpose, whether I am aware of it or not.

Love Embraces All

"Love is the only reality and it is not a mere sentiment. It is the ultimate truth that lies at the heart of creation." Rabindranth Tagore (1861-1941)

Animals and children are the innocent examples of unconditional love because they are pure, empty of ideas imparted by others. It is when we start getting older that we pick up the judgments, prejudices, and fears of the adults in our lives.

One aspect of Love is the ability to keep our hearts open by releasing ourselves from all judgments: "I am right, you are wrong. How could you think this way? Why are you spreading fear?" We all are doing the best we can with our level of awareness. It is in this diversity that keeps us learning from one another and above all learning about ourselves. It is easy to be loving and kind when the way is smooth, but when tested, how do we react? Do we lash out in order to hurt, or do we introspect and grow from the experience?

When we step down from the elevated platform of judgment, the tightness that judgment places in one's heart and overall energy simply leaves, and from this state of being we can take action, be it inspiring another, extending healing, or being an agent of change.

It takes a loving daily practice, a conscious intention of sincerely looking at ourselves, in order to let go of that which creates separation from one another.

I began to understand that I was better off letting go of what I believed, and, instead, to stand naked in front of the ocean of life.

The Naked Truth

"Your duty is to BE and not be this or that." — *Ramana Maharshi (1879-1950)*

I reached a point when my heart ached for an understanding of this thing called life. I didn't want answers given to me by authorities telling me what I should or should not believe in. I didn't need more methods or rituals to help me to understand, or made-up stories of where I originally came from. I had tried them all, and I still didn't have a deep knowledge of who or what God was. I began to understand that I was better off letting go of what I believed, and, instead, to stand naked in front of the ocean of life. Perhaps in allowing myself to be the ocean, free from preconceived ideas, I would experience the totality of my being and come face-to-face with God at last.

Soul's Longing

"Whatever the soul longs for will be attained by the Spirit." — *Khalil Gibran (1883-1931)*

There often can be a deep longing within that breaks one's heart. Neither tears nor joy can fill the gap, nor the surrounding of loved ones, as they are but temporary guests in one's life. It's not a longing of unfulfilled dreams; it's an emptiness that gives a glimpse that we are more than what our senses tells us, or the roles we carry in life's journey. We are immortality Itself, and until we wake up to this awareness, the ache within will be a constant reminder we have temporally forgotten our divine nature.

Trusting the Perfection of the Universe

"All things happen for a reason, even though it's an eternity sometimes before we learn those reasons." – Author unknown

I didn't understand, for a long time, how the statements everything happens for a reason, or there is perfection in the universe, could be valid. The world seemed chaotic and often cruel. How could a tsunami, earthquakes, fires, or man's inhumanity to man be perfect? I could see perfection in the things that would bring love, peace, joy, and beauty into the world.

I did not realize then, that if we pay very close attention to the events in our personal lives, no matter how challenging, it can lead to transformations in our lives. The pieces, like a puzzle, fit together to create the person you have become. Upon reflection you may realize that if it were not for the challenges in your life, you wouldn't have had the motivation to realize your potential, to let go of what no longer works in your life, or become more compassionate or stronger. Oftentimes, when faced with challenges, we develop a greater spiritual depth and appreciation for the sacredness of life.

Our human mind can never understand the reason for certain events in our world and where the exact perfection is, such as in the death of a loved one, but your spirit, which is the truth of who we are, understands your existence.

Stilling the mind, seeing through a higher intuition, allows for a knowing of the perfection of the universe to start becoming breathtakingly clear.

Recognizing the World is But an Illusion

"Be in the world, but not of it." John 17:15-17

The spiritual quote depending on your spiritual focus, *"Be in the world, but not of it,"* reminds us we are spiritual beings having a human experience. We are not the mind/body that operates in the world, we are Awareness/God/ expressing Itself as a human being. This made my eyes a little wet, because I was thinking that these spiritual truths have been shared by sages throughout the centuries, in different wording but the same message, and yet mankind still suffers. The Buddha reminds us:

"A wise man, recognizing that the world is but an illusion, does not act as if it is real, so he escapes the suffering."

It's now the 21st century, and many of us fail to recognize that the true essence of life is our infinite nature which contains the purity of love. It is this purity that delights in the experience of life. Instead of focusing on separation, possessions, and wars over land and religion, our true nature knows it's all an illusion weaved by the mind of humanity. *It knows its true essence is love.*

How simple it all is, if we but keep our minds and hearts open and finally have the courage to listen.

*Feel the rhythm of your breath as you inhale and exhale.
Feel infinity touching your face.*

Infinity's Touch

"Practice not-doing. And everything will fall into place." – Tao Te Ching

Close your eyes and be still. Feel the rhythm of your breath as you inhale and exhale. Feel infinity touching your face. There is no struggle, or trying to make things work, just an endless flow of divine movement; a movement that is always creative. This movement gives us all that is contained in experience: our birth, life, and death. Being attuned to this flow frees us, helps us to be awake to the nuances and the whispers the universe is communicating. In this endless movement, we can be in touch with the immortality of our spirit.

This is living fully present with yourself, in touch with your Divinity.

*The universe, the very air that we breathe,
is infused with God.*

Listening to the Whispers

"I love to think of nature as an unlimited broadcasting station, through which God speaks to us every hour, if we will only tune in." – George Washington Carver (1864-1943)

When seeking guidance or healing, often the answer to one's prayers or intentions come from the earth itself. The universe, the very air that we breathe, is infused with God. There is nothing that is not God; even sorrow has the touch of divinity in it.

The universe is alive, communicating with all of its creations, but if we close our minds in fear or doubt, we may miss the gentle whisper of the Divine. When we have an openness and listen with our heart we will connect to the daily inspiration that divinity is communicating to us. Why not? The Divine enjoys all forms of creation, and communication is a creative opportunity for the Creator's expression. It can be in the form of a bird landing on your windowsill, a chance encounter with a stranger, or even a radio announcement that has a message can be of guidance.

We are all connected, the creatures of the earth and ocean, the trees, the flowers, our brothers and sisters. We are all messengers for one another. We are not alone.

On Having a Hearing Challenge

"The marvelous richness of human experience would lose something of rewarding joy if there were no limitations to overcome." Helen Keller (A deaf-blind American author, activist and lecturer - 1880-1968)

Now that I am older, living with my soulmate, working from home, and engaging in creative projects, living a peaceful and loving life, I look back and think that if I came face-to-face with God and He asked me, "If you could begin again, would you have wanted to hear normally?" My answer would be, "No." Everything in life shapes us, not just the challenges to our body and senses, but the love we have won and lost, the tears, the joy – even the moments when our trust may have been betrayed.

Because of my hearing disability, I became more compassionate, perhaps kinder. My sixth sense became acutely attuned to the world around me and beyond. It gave me depth and a psychological awareness of others I may have missed out on otherwise. But now I'm at a stage where, when I set goals, it's for my spiritual awareness, personal empowerment, or simply for fun. I'm not the person of my younger years whose focus was to prove something to myself and others and to feed my ego. So if God asked me now, "Do you want to hear now?" I would respond, "Yes." I would love to hear a bird's song, the rustle of the wind, or the tones of music I lost the ability to hear at age 33. I want to be able to converse freely with every human being on the planet. It would add a new dimension to my life experience, a joyful one, one of discovery.

I would like to hear. But if it should not happen in this lifetime, I will embrace the path.

Recapturing Our Childlike Joy

The great man is he who does not lose his childlike heart."
Mencius (Chinese Philosopher - 372–289 BCE)

I took a walk alone into town on a sunny day and sat down for a few minutes to watch children play at a local park. What joy and innocence! They were squealing with delight, faces flushed from running and eyes wide open with anticipation for their next game of make-believe. I then saw an older girl, maybe 12, more serious than the others. But she smiled at me as she walked past. She's growing up, I thought, taking on the heaviness and seriousness that being an adult entails for most.

I tried to pinpoint when I had lost the joy of my childhood, that time when laughter was exhilarating and the world was a playground. I would go to sleep with anticipation for the fun I would have with my friends the following day. I realized that the heaviness descended upon me when I began to perceive the world as a frightening place, when I experienced loss, when school became a challenge, and when I wasn't allowed to be myself because it was considered "wrong" by the well-meaning adults around me: my parents, family, and teachers.

We begin to lose our childhood joy when we become self-conscious, fearful of expressing ourselves. When we bow to the pressures exerted by the mores of our culture, it stifles the soul. The creatures of the earth are always themselves. Perhaps they can teach us to be.

Surrender and Release

"To hold, you must first open your hand. Let go." Lao Tzu
(c.604 - 531 B.C.)

We live in a world of duality. Because of this, we continually experience cycles of growth and cycles when life slows down and presents us with challenges. It's not the challenging situation that matters, it's how we deal with it and perceive it. How attached are we to wanting things to be a certain way? It is this attachment that causes suffering.

As an example, when I accepted in my mind and heart that I was no longer employable in the corporate world of New York due to the economic adjustments and other factors after 9/11, I felt a burden lift. Soon after, doors started to open, and I found alternate ways to earn a living.

The release of this attachment led to my state of surrender and acceptance. I accepted that some situations can't be changed, but also learned how I could create new opportunities to replace what had been lost. I could go on living, while I did what had to be done. This often involved asking for help. I learned from this experience that allowing myself to wallow in fear and drama only complicated the situation. This kind of behavior throws off our balance and clouds our judgment.

When confronting fear with trust, inspiration often leads the way.

Compassion - A Lesson for The Day

"In separateness lies the world's great misery, in compassion lies the world's true strength." Buddha

In our household, we have a set of angel cards. Each has a one-word spiritual attribute printed on it. My soul mate, Phil, and I take turns selecting a card in the morning before starting our day. We pay attention and see how the message may express itself in our day.

One morning I chose one at random: "Compassion." On that day, I was in a hurry. I needed to pick up an item at a department store, so I took a comfortable twenty-minute bus ride into town. I enjoyed the scenery of our semi-rural town, the warmth of the female bus driver and the coziness of pleasant weather.

On the way back, after getting out of the store in less than fifteen minutes, I was met with a challenge. This time the bus driver was a cranky, older man who I happened to notice had a hearing disability. The ride was bumpy and scary. Besides driving faster than he should have, he took out a piece of gum and unwrapped it slowly, both his hands lifted from the steering wheel. He then aimed the wrap at the garbage can next to the door and grumbled because he missed. I remembered once before when I had the same unpleasant experience with his driving and his demeanor. As we neared my stop I pulled the bell cord, but he didn't hear it, so I missed my stop. When he saw me get up he asked, "You get off here?" Calmly I replied, "Yes." I didn't say anything about my missed stop and, instead, simply wished him a good day.

Walking back home, I engaged in negative mental chatter: "This man really shouldn't be driving! An accident could have happened! He needs an attitude makeover." Then I remembered the word on the angel card. I also have a hearing disability, though I hoped I came off as more pleasant than this gentleman. The minute I felt compassion, not pity, I came to an understanding that in the journey of life we all are doing the best we can. Having a handicap makes that even more difficult. My heart opened and my mind relaxed instantly. I don't think this is empathy. I would have come to the same understanding even if he didn't have a hearing challenge. What a shift! I could once again enjoy the soft breeze and the clear blue skies.

Webster's dictionary defines compassion as "Sympathetic consciousness of others' distress, together with a desire to alleviate it." Compassion is expressed in different forms: attitude, service, and action. When we reach out to help someone in need, even if it is to lend a friendly shoulder to lean on, we are alleviating suffering. When we keep our mind still without falling into judgment, we are also being compassionate.

I have an open heart, so it's not difficult for me to live a life of compassion. But the lesson I learned that day was about compassionate understanding of a higher order. In my life, I have been the recipient of different forms of compassion, and for that I'm grateful. The mind is generally busy judging and over-dramatizing as I did that day on the bus. This is what creates separation, whereas the heart simply knows and acts accordingly, often without fear.

In life we need to have love and compassion not only for the world, but also for ourselves and have understanding for another. This unconditional understanding is not of the mind but of the heart. It is an acceptance that we are all part of the human condition and the illusion of life. No matter who we are or where we are, the attributes of love – one of which is compassion – are what truly matter in the end.

Death – A Temporary Separation

Live your life that the fear of death can never enter your heart. Trouble no one about their religion; respect others in their views, and demand that they respect yours.

Love your life, perfect your life, beautify all things in your life. Seek to make your life long and of service to your people. Prepare a noble death song for the day when you go over the great divide.

Always give a word or sign of salute when meeting or passing a stranger if in a lonely place. Show respect to all people, but grovel to none. When you arise in the morning, give thanks for the light, for your life and strength. Give thanks for your food and for the joy of living. If you see no reason for giving thanks, the fault lies in yourself.

When your time comes to die, be not like those whose hearts are filled with fear of death, so that when their time comes they weep and pray for a little more time to live their lives over again in a different way.

Sing your death song, and die like a hero going home.

Chief Tecumseh (Crouching Tiger) Shawnee Nation - 1768-1813

Beyond Inspiration

This poem is in honor of my nephew Omar, who is now our teenage angel.

"I am Your Angel

*Now that I am in the other world
where souls find a resting place
among the rainbow colored waterfalls -
I will be your guardian angel
your sweet angel watching over you.*

*I will dry your tears
and hold you in a tight embrace
and your heart will remember
I am only a tender breath away.*

*You can call me when your heart is breaking
you can call me when you want to feel my love
you can call me and I will be by your side
even if I am now dancing in the Light with God.*

*I may seem to be gone but
I am still with you
while we fulfill God's Higher Plan.
I am a tender breath away
always loving you...*

Death has a way of separating us physically but never severing the bond of love.

Spirit Speaking

Let children walk with Nature, let them see the beautiful blending and communions of death and life, their joyous inseparable unity, as taught in woods and meadows, plains and mountains, and streams of our blessed star, and they learn that death is stingless indeed, and as beautiful as life. John Muir (1938-1914)

God speaks to us in the wind that blows, in the rise and fall of the ocean's waves, in the song of a bird, in the crimson colors of a sunset dancing across the sky, nature's masterpiece to behold. It is in moments like these I cannot fathom that my loved ones have ceased to be; they live on as part of God's world though in a form I do not yet see. They live on in my memories and heart, and one day we shall meet again.

Loss of Child

"When someone you love becomes a memory, the memory becomes a treasure." – Author Unknown

When a young one suddenly leaves our side, they stay forever frozen in time in our minds and hearts. The years go by, and as they remain eternally young in our memories, we wonder how their lives would have turned out. Would they have fulfilled their dreams? What would their children have looked like had they started a family? It is as if a light has been turned off – the light of youthful dreams. Yet if we close our eyes and listen with our hearts, we will not only remember our young one, but feel their eternal love.

Death has a way of separating us physically but never

severing the bond of love. They are alive in our hearts, around us in spirit, often thanking us eternally as souls for the roles we had in their brief physical experience.

Openings and Connection

"Perhaps they are not stars, but openings in the Heaven, Where the love of our lost ones pours through and shines down upon us, To let us know they are happy" – *Author Unknown*

When our world is turned upside down by the death of a loved one, the grief often peels layers from us – the layers of pretending we are stronger than we are, of pretending we are now immune to mankind's inhumanity. It opens our heart to feel an even deeper empathy for the sorrow that another human being may be experiencing; it can make us more aware of our connection to the universe and to be in gratitude for the simplest pleasures of our day-to-day living. We are reminded of how fragile life can be, and how things can change in an instant. Yet, in this fragility we can sense the power is not in our humanity, but in something deeper within and beyond that the eye and the mind cannot yet perceive.

Death and Rebirth

"Death is as sure for that which is born, as birth is for that which is dead. Therefore grieve not for what is inevitable." – *Bhagavad Gita*

I am humbled to be reminded by ancient writings, many from cultures that are different from mine, of the promise that we all survive the discarding of our bodies and of rebirth. It gives me a sense of a sacred continuity that not even the advancements of civilization have been able to touch.

Impermanence

"Thus shall you think of all this fleeting world: A star at dawn, a bubble in a stream, a flash of lightening in a summer cloud, a flickering lamp, a phantom,, and a dream." – Diamond Sutra

Nothing in this world is permanent, not our material possessions, jobs, home, relationships or our physicality; everything comes to an end at some point, like the star at dawn disappearing into the great mystery that is called life. Yet instead of fearing this impermanence, which is in essence little births and deaths, we can ask what is it that is permanent, and one can get a sense it's the part of us that knows the Source, and that is our souls. Being aware of this, I have faith I shall meet my loved again one day.

Transformation

"Deep, unspeakable suffering may well be called a baptism, a regeneration, the initiation into a new state. Suffering can be likened to a baptism - the passing over the threshold of pain and grief and anguish to claim a new state of being." – George Eliot (1819-1880)

We are never the same after a loss or deep suffering, but it's often surprising to find that when we thought we could not cope, that we would not see the sun shine again, we emerge a different person who draws strength from a place deep within that has always been with us, but may not have been noticed before. This is the place that is not touched by our humanity. It's the place where the Eternal dwells.

We can ask what is it that is permanent, and one can get a sense it's the part of us that knows the Source, and that is our souls.

Behind the Veil

"After your death, you will be what you were before birth."
Arthur Schopenhauer (German Philosopher) 1788-1860

Sometimes we may wonder how anyone can truly know if our loved ones are really behind the veil, what proof there is that the soul survives physical death. After all, those who make any pronouncements about death and the afterlife are alive. It's similar to the doubt that may arise in some people about the existence of God. Just because things cannot be seen or touched does not mean they do not exist. We cannot see electricity or the wind, yet we experience their effects. It takes faith that as God exists in whatever concept we have of God, the soul, which is energy, also exists and lives on forever, since energy never perishes. We feel the effects of the realm behind the veil whenever we experience a sense of deep peace that is not of this world, or notice a sign that gives us a us a glimpse that a loved one we are mourning is actually alive and well behind the veil.

Flying Free

When the heart weeps for what it has lost, the soul laughs for what it has found. Sufi aphorism

I'm often intrigued by how the majority of literature – religious, spiritual, or philosophical – often portrays death as a joyful liberation for the soul. When we hear of loved ones visiting from beyond this world or have dreams about them, we sense that the departed are happy, free from whatever challenges they confronted during earthly life. How can death be joyful even for those who had happy lives? I conclude, not with my finite mind but with my heart and a higher part of me, that the dead are joyful because existing without a physical body is like growing wings that enable us to fly free at last and reach our true Home.

Closure

There are things that we don't want to happen but have to accept, things we don't want to know but have to learn, and people we can't live without but have to let go. ~Author Unknown

Closure carries a different meaning for each individual. The circumstances surrounding the passing of a loved one and the deceased's relationship to the living one are unique to each situation. For one person, closure in dealing with the crossing over of a loved one may mean surrendering to their concept of God and trusting that the loved one is in a better place. For another person, it may mean learning to live life in a different way, even if there is an emptiness created by the one who left that can never be filled. Some say there is never closure when it comes to loss, just a moving forward and an acceptance of life's destiny.

Life is a series of beginnings and endings, openings and closings, some that gladden the spirit and others that challenge it. We cannot grow without these contrasts.

We experience a sense of peace when we assign meaning to the passing of a loved one. It helps to keep the memory alive and it allows closure to become easier.

Planting a tree or creating a beautiful space in a garden where you can sit and meditate, opening a website that will inspire others, painting, writing, or establishing a foundation in honor of a loved one are all ways of channeling your grief in a healthier direction. It allows for the transmutation of grief.

    Don't allow grief to dim the light of your spirit. Let your spirit shine brightly in honor of yourself and your loved one, and trust that at some point peace will be found.

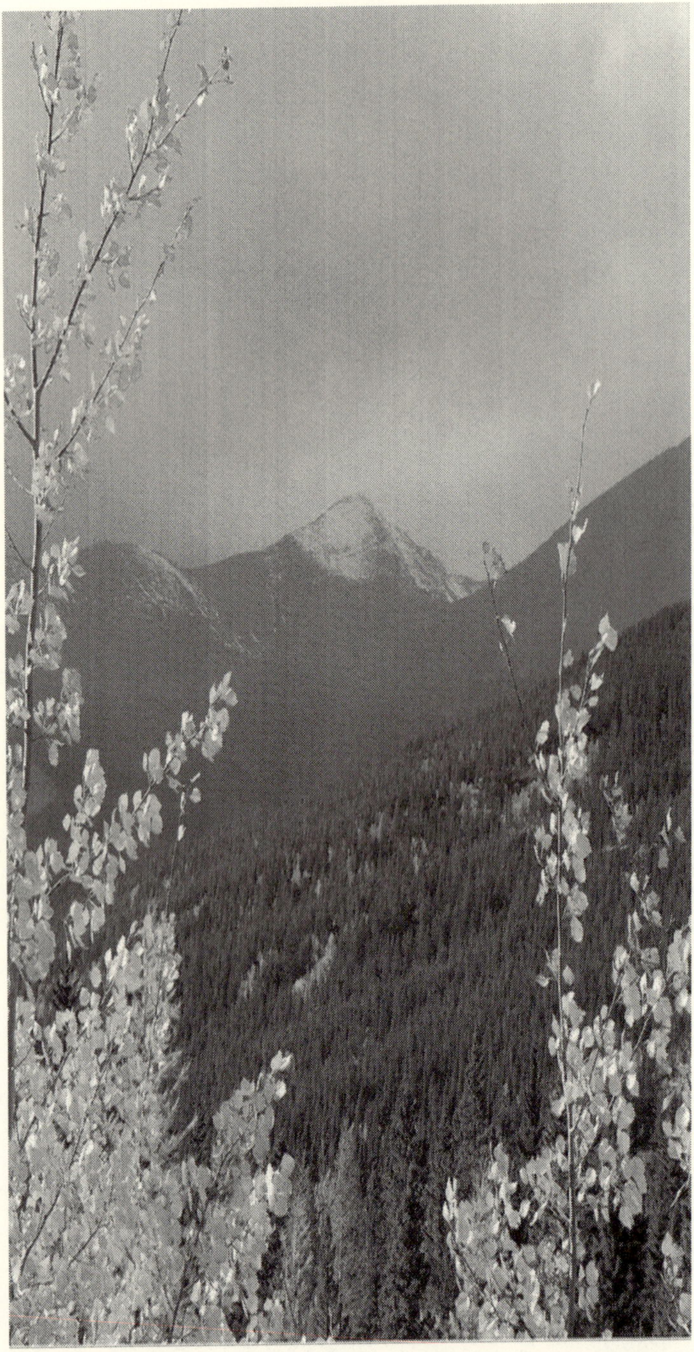

Nature's Lessons

They will come back, come back again.
As long as the red Earth rolls.
He never wasted a leaf or a tree.
Do you think He would squander souls?"
Rudyard Kipling (1865-1936)

On a cool, wet, and quiet autumn afternoon, strolling in the park with my soul mate, we noticed the changing colors of the leaves. While we admired their beauty, it dawned on us that as these leaves died and fell to the ground in varying shades of brown, red, and gold, their deaths were beautiful, an essential part of nature's cycle, and they would be reborn the following spring. There is no struggle in nature with death. It is humans who struggle with the fear of it. If nature is in harmony with death and rebirth, why should it be any different for us? We are, after all, part of nature and, like the leaves falling off a tree, we discard our bodies and come back again and again, since the spirit never dies.

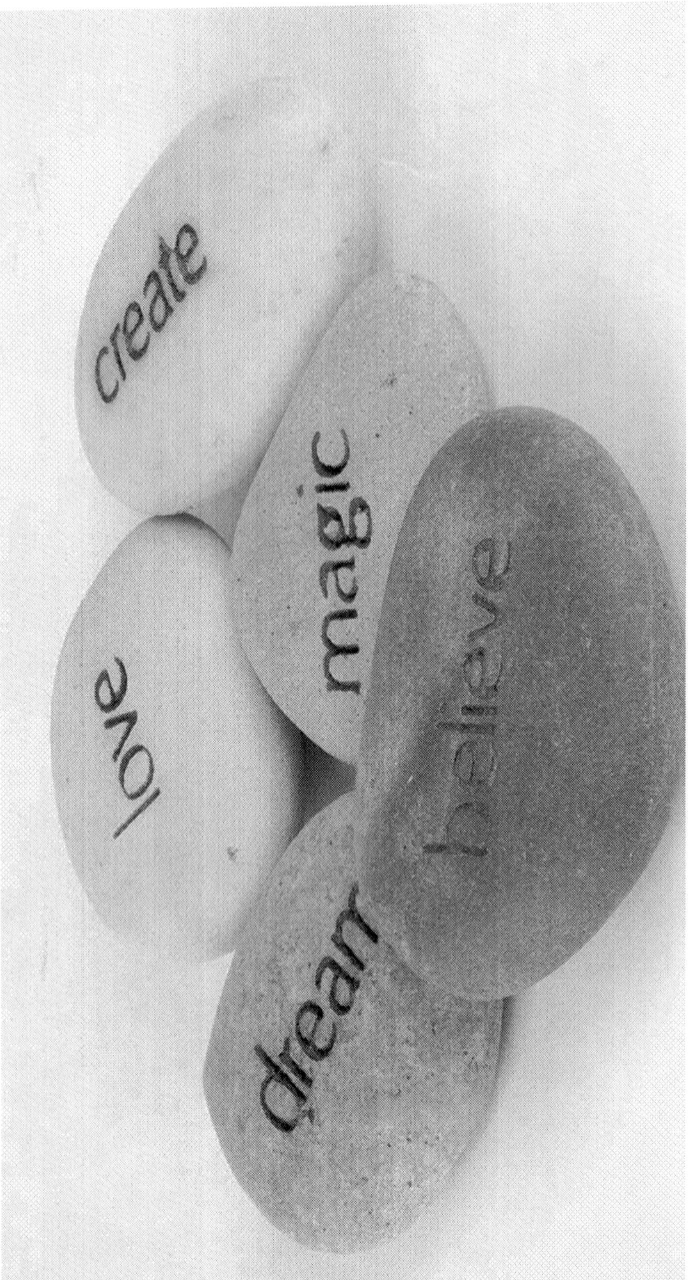
create
love
magic
believe
dream

Inspire My Day Affirmations

The use of affirmations is a wonderful tool, one that is not new in the world of psychology or spirituality. It attracts men and women from all walks of life who wonder what the limitations and potential are in repeating words over and over again in actually creating change in their lives.

Are affirmations magical words? Do they really manifest money, a car, or the healing of a challenge? Or the change in one's spiritual awareness? Not by themselves; we need to work on our inner selves as well.

We attract what we want to experience into our lives by changing what we feel. The feelings we have around the memories of the events in our lives – the traumas, the fears, the disappointments, especially in childhood – are the vibrations that broadcast to the universe what we think we are worthy and capable of receiving.

Affirmations help you move your focus from self-defeating thoughts to higher ones that support not only your goals but your health.

Scientists are finding that the brain has the capacity to alter its structure. The brain does not know the difference between imagination and reality. If we pretend to play a musical instrument, images of a brain PET scan (Positron Emission Tomography) is almost identical as the one taken when we are literally playing the musical instrument. This is exciting news, as the brain influences our health and quality of life.

A scientist, Dr. Masuro Emoto* has done extensive research on how feelings and thoughts modify the basic structure of water; words such as "hate" and "love" result in different crystal formations which he has photographed. He has written several books with photographs that give tangible proof that thoughts have power. We are composed of water, so think how your thoughts are affecting you!

You can repeat the affirmations that follow daily, or select one at random, or one that resonates with you. As you repeat the affirmations, also take a few minutes during the day or before bedtime to visualize yourself happy, healthy, and doing what you wish to be or accomplish, but do not forget to also work with your inner self. You deserve it!

Attachments
I now take a deep breath, and I am open to releasing attachment to memories that are blocking my progress.

Doing what I Love
I live my life doing what I love, which enriches my soul.

---

*Dr. Masuro Emoto: "The Hidden Messages in Water"

Creating My Day
*I am grateful for the opportunity to express
love, compassion and kindness,
and to add beauty
to my world each day.*

Magnificence
*Everything that I desire comes easily to me,
and I enjoy a life filled
with magnificence!*

Wholeness
*Everyday I connect to the energy of wholeness
and every day my body is responding
to my healthy thoughts.*

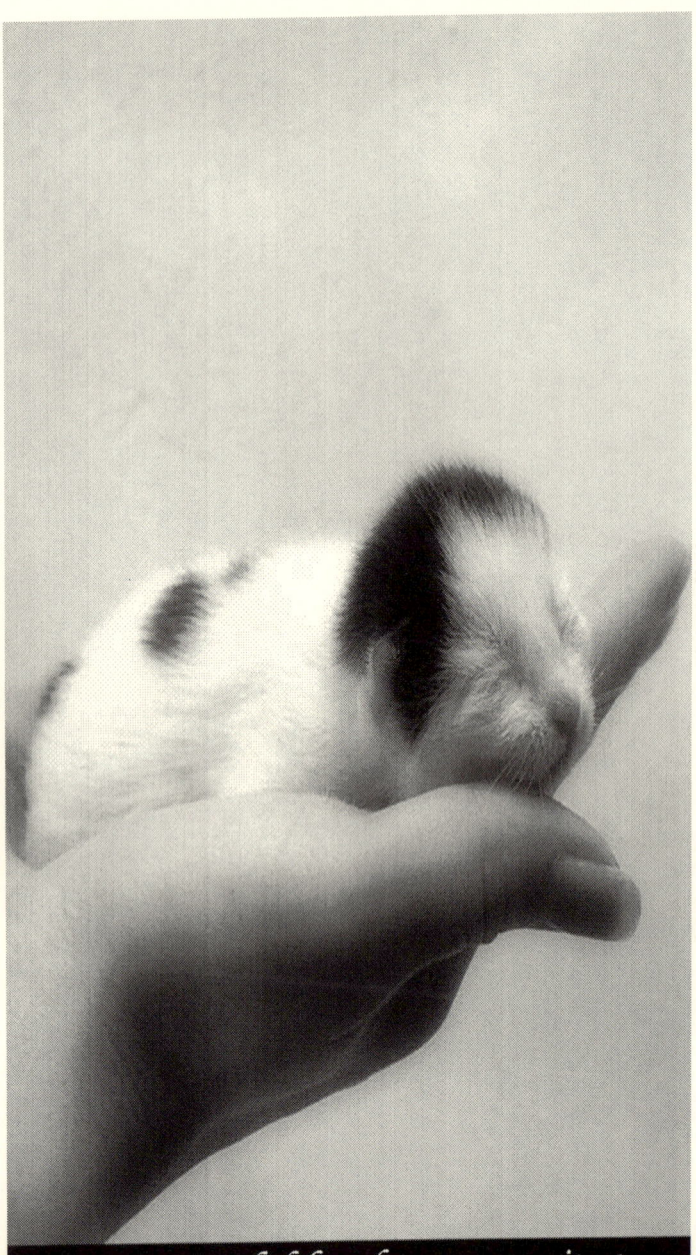

I am grateful for the opportunity to express love, compassion, and kindness.

Wisdom
Wisdom is the compass that
guides me in the journey
of my life.

Honoring Life
Life is a sacred opportunity
for experience and growth.
I honor this gift.

Abundance
Abundance is now part of my life
because my thoughts and feelings
are focused on
abundance,
and what I feel within,
I attract.

Breath is life. I breathe in love, I breathe out love.

The Breath of Life
Breath is life.
I breathe in love,
I breathe out love.
I breathe in peace,
I breathe out peace.
I am one with the universe.

Magic of Life
I am in perfect
alignment with my higher self
and have a deep
appreciation for the magic of life.

Supportive People
I live in a friendly universe,
and the Law of Attraction
brings supportive people
into my life.
I am joyful and blessed
by this connection.

Allowing Joy
I have faith in the power of my divine spirit
and allow joy to enter my life
by consciously making choices
that honor my mind, body, and spirit.

I am Calm
I connect to the Infinite Stillness
within me.
I am calm, at peace, in the flow.
All is well in my world.

Committing to Goals
I commit to my goals and rejoice
in seeing the blossoming
of what I wish to achieve in my life.

Marie Jiménez-Beaumont

Healthy Body
My body welcomes harmony and balance,
therefore I make healthy choices
that nourish every
tissue, cell, and organ of
my magnificent body.

Unique Divine Expression
I am a divine expression -
With a unique purpose
in this world.
I completely
love and accept myself.

Higher Voice
When making choices or decisions,
I listen to the
voice of inspiration and not fear.

The infinite field of possibilities is open to me.

Infinite Field of Possibilities
The infinite field of possibilities
is open to me
as I fill my mind and heart
with belief and gratitude
for Creation's opportunities.

Forgiveness
As I release all past traumas
I am free from resentments and regrets.
The past has no hold on me,
and I now move forward with
an open heart
filled with peace.

In the Moment
Love, joy, and peace are flourishing in my life
as I learn to live in
the moment,
away from mind's spinning.

I am free from resentments and regrets.

Self-Trust

Self-trust is the inner spark
that ignites
my ability to express
my wondrous potential.

Mind, Body, and Spirit Renewal

Each new day I am reborn
and I take this opportunity to
renew my mind, body, and spirit.
I entertain thoughts of
love and goodwill,
and exercise and nourish my body
in healthy ways.

*I move in the direction of freedom
from self-created limitations.*

Freedom from Limitations
*I move in the direction of
freedom from self-created limitations.
The universe is limitless and
I align myself to this wellspring
of abundance, opportunity, and growth.*

Greatness of Spirit
*I surrender not to smallness but
to the innate grandeur of my Spirit.
I rejoice in this ever-expansive
connection and expression of
all I can be and do in
the journey of my life.*

Clear Path
*The past is gone, the future is not yet formed.
I embrace the moment fully,
and this moves my life forward
with a clear path.*

Bounty of the Universe
I am a child of the universe,
no less than the trees and stars.
I deserve the
bounty of the universe
and I am deeply grateful.

Mind and Heart Agreeing
If my mind and heart agree,
I can move mountains
and lead the life
I envision and deserve.

Releasing Limiting Thoughts
What is going on within me is reflected in
the life outside of me.
I work on releasing limiting thoughts.

Marie Jiménez-Beaumont

Miracles
I tune in to the presence of miracles
and watch how my life
can be transformed into a glorious experience.

Self-Love
As I learn to love myself,
I treat myself with
kindness and respect.
I am a valuable, infinite being
with a unique purpose
in the grand scheme of life.
I now walk with a deep appreciation
of who I am and return
this love to others.

I realize the futility of hanging onto what no longer empowers me or feeds my soul.

Soothe Your Soul Meditations

As we become more attuned to our inner selves, we become aware of the infinite Intelligence that is inherent in all of life. Instead of running in opposition to life with the chaos of our mental spinning, we can become present as the creatures of nature are, and who do not struggle to have their needs met by the universe. We start to get into the flow, feeling supported by the infinite source of life.

These short, spiritual, meditative thoughts are helpful in bringing your focus inward – perhaps you can read them in your meditation space and ponder the words. The more we focus on Truth and letting go of ideas that no longer serve us, the more open we become to creating shifts in our awareness. We start seeing the world through new eyes. A favorite English poet of mine sums it up well:

If the doors to perception were cleansed, everything will be seen as it is, infinite. – William Blake

Truth is simple; it is the human mind that complicates it.

Stillness
There is a light in all of Creation that
is there for me to embrace
if I but silence my thoughts
and allow the silence to be my beacon.
There is power in stillness.

Nature Speaks

God speaks to me through the
trees, creatures, and colors of nature.
I now choose to listen,
not only with my mind, but also with my heart.

The Eagles' Gift

Observing the beauty of an eagle
in its graceful flight,
I realize the futility of hanging onto
what no longer empowers me or feeds my soul.
I set myself free.

Expressions of One Source

I stand in awe of the expressions of the One Source.
All the love and fear just developing and
disappearing —
everything is in a constant state of change.
What a magical ride!

Marie Jiménez-Beaumont

Simplifying

The more I simplify my life by
letting go of
old ideas, fears, and attachments,
the more profoundly attuned I become to
the natural rhythm that is in all of life.

We Are Love

From Love we come and to Love we return.
This is not a mere sentiment, but
the ultimate Truth at the heart of creation.
My open heart is immersed in
the fragrance of God's Love.

Beauty's Love Song

Outward physical beauty is a pleasure to see,
but the light in our heart is God's masterpiece.
I am in touch with my inner beauty, God's
love song.

Gratitude expands my heart. Suddenly, a dark sky comes alive with dancing stars.

Gratitude

Gratitude expands my heart.
Suddenly, a dark sky comes alive with dancing stars,
reminding me
I am the star,
I am the wind whispering,
I am the gentle touch of love.

Present Moment

The present moment is the only reality that exists.
The past is gone and the future is not yet formed.
When living in the moment,
all of life becomes a potential for wonder.

God's Creative Expression

Once we understand that all of life is a myrad of God's creative expression,
we become less attached,
as both the negative and positive
spring from the same Source.

Dance and Dancer
Nothing is separate, nothing is alone.
We are the dance and the dancer.
If we awaken to who we truly are,
what joy it is to know we are
deathless, endless, and free.

Soul's Prompting
We cannot be fully aware of the beauty of
our soul's prompting
until we have tasted silence
by calming the
incessant chatter of the mind.

Impermanent World
If we are to find permanence in
an impermanent world,
where all objects come and go,
let us seek to be aware of the Self,
which is permanent and infinite.

Marie Jiménez-Beaumont

Ego's Need

When you drop the ego's need
for approval or to impress,
you create a space for authenticity.
Embracing your true self
will make you a witness to
your infinite potential.

Yielding Heart

A soft, yielding heart holds the promise of
experiencing life with strength and depth.
A tree that does not bend
will crack in the wind;
what is soft can be strong.

Equanimity

Equanimity is an eternal Stillness,
our true source,
a light that remains a constant
during the ebb and tide of life.
We find it by revealing our true nature.

Life's Song
The whispering wind, the song of a bird,
the sound of rushing water, music playing:
what a symphony life gives us
if we but stop to listen with open hearts.

Surrender
When we give up the need to control everything,
to struggle with what is
and trust in the natural movement of life,
we are free.

Experiencing the God in You
In order to awaken to the
radiance of your spirit,
all that is necessary is to
turn to the conscious
silence within that
is fully awake to God.

Marie Jiménez-Beaumont

Duality

Life's duality brings light and darkness,
joy and sorrow,
all divine expressions for the
soul's experience.
I am always evolving.

Kindness

Kindness is a light that
shines a ray of hope,
opens the heart,
and graces the soul.

Greatness of Our Spirit

What joy is to be aware we are
not "worms of the Earth," but
magnificent beings, roaming the Earth.
We need to surrender not to our smallness
but to the greatness of our spirit.

In the silence of the distance the ocean's strength speaks to me.

The Ocean's Gift

In the silence of the distance,
the ocean's strength
speaks to me,
reminding me that
inner strength
can arise by calming
the space of my mind.

Reflection

I create my reality from the inside out.
The thoughts I harbor within
reflect in the world outside of me,
the one I experience.
Of my thoughts I choose to be conscious.

Divine Unfolding

I am a child of the universe,
everything in my life is
unfolding in divine perfection,
even if my human side
does not yet understand.

The cosmic dance of creation brings forth a never-ending cycle of birth, life and rebirth.

Cosmic Dance
The cosmic dance of creation
brings forth a never-ending cycle of
birth, life, and rebirth.
Every day I am reborn
as I let go of ideas that
hide the Truth of my divinity.

Silencing Mind's Chatter
We cannot be fully aware of the
beauty of our soul's prompting,
until we have tasted silence
by calming the incessant
chatter of the mind.

Love
Love is simply creation's
greatest joy,
the life of the soul;
when we love,
we know God.

Personal Notes

Personal Notes

Personal Notes

APPENDIX

The following list of resources can be used for inspiration and the nurturing of your mind, body and spirit. Several have a physical address, others are online spiritual communities that embrace all paths.

Agape International Spiritual Center
Founded by Dr. Michael Bernard Beckwith
(Agape is a trans-denominational spiritual "center" that honors our divinity and oneness)
5700 Buckingham Parkway
Culver City, CA 90230
(310) 348-1250
Website: http://www.agapelive.com/

A Course in Miracles (ACIM)
Is a self-study spiritual thought system that teaches the way to Universal Love through forgiveness.
Website: http://acim.org/

Daily OM
(Nurturing Mind, Body and Spirit)
A diverse spiritual community where you can join the conversations, take courses and make new friends.
Website: http://www.dailyom.com/

New York Open Center
(Largest holistic learning center in the United States)
22 East 30th Street New York
New York, NY 10016-7002
(212) 219-2527
Website: http://www.opencenter.org/

Omega Institute
(Supports wellness for mind, body and spirit)
260 Lake Drive
Rhinebeck, NY 12572-3212
Call Toll free 877.944.2002 (US)
Website: http://eomega.org/

Positively Positive –(Your Attitude +Your choices =Your Life)
At its core, the message is about optimism and inspiration. It has swept the globe and has over 1 million fans.
Website: http://www.positivelypositive.com/

Silent Unity
(A spiritual organization to ask for prayers 24/7. All paths to God are honored.)
888-919-5752
Website: www.unityonline.org

Spiritual Networks
(World's Largest Spiritual Social Network and Online Community)
Website: www.spiritualnetworks.com

The World Peace Prayer Society
(May Peace Prevail on Earth)
An organization that acknowledges that words and thoughts affect the energy field of our planet.
Website: http://www.worldpeace.org/

TUT – Notes from the Universe
(Delightful site that helps dreams come true with positive messages)
Website: http://www.tut.com/theclub/

Biography

Marie Jiménez-Beaumont is an intuitive counselor with over 25 years of experience. She co-owns a health website, thelemonadediet.com, with her spouse, Phil. The Lemonade Diet is a program created by naturopath Stanley Burroughs over 70 years ago. It helps detoxify the body while losing weight.

Marie's journey led her from the bright, high-paced life of New York, where she had lived most of her life, to the serenity of a semi-rural town in Oregon where she spends most of her time writing and assisting others with her intuitive gifts.

If you wish to contact her, she can be reached at:
Beyondinspirationnow@yahoo.com

Beyond Inspiration
Marie Jiménez-Beaumont

Made in the USA
Lexington, KY
06 March 2012